MOMENTS WITH ONESELF SERIES: 7

PURPOSE OF PRAYER

SWAMI DAYANANDA SARASWATI

ARSHA VIDYA

ARSHA VIDYA
RESEARCH AND PUBLICATION TRUST
CHENNAI

Published by :
Arsha Vidya Research
and Publication Trust
32 / 4 ' Sri Nidhi ' Apts III Floor
Sir Desika Road Mylapore
Chennai 600 004 INDIA
Tel   : 044 2499 7023
Telefax: 2499 7131
Email : avrandpc@gmail.com

ISBN : 978 - 81 - 904203 - 3 - 4

Revised Edition : August   2007   Copies : 2000
1st Reprint   : May   2009   Copies : 1000
2nd Reprint   : November   2010   Copies : 2000

Design :
Graaphic Design

Printed by :
Sudarsan Graphics
27, Neelakanta Mehta Street
T. Nagar, Chennai 600 017
Email : info@sudarsan.com

CONTENTS

KEY TO TRANSLITERATION AND PRONUNCIATION OF
SANSKRIT LETTERS

Sanskrit is a highly phonetic language and hence accuracy in articulation of the letters is important. For those unfamiliar with the *Devanāgari* script, the international transliteration is a guide to the proper pronunciation of Sanskrit letters.

अ	a	(but)	ट	ṭa	(true)*3
आ	ā	(father)	ठ	ṭha	(anthill)*3
इ	i	(it)	ड	ḍa	(drum)*3
ई	ī	(beat)	ढ	ḍha	(godhead)*3
उ	u	(full)	ण	ṇa	(under)*3
ऊ	ū	(pool)	त	ta	(path)*4
ऋ	ṛ	(rhythm)	थ	tha	(thunder)*4
ॠ	ṝ	(marine)	द	da	(that)*4
ऌ	ḷ	(revelry)	ध	dha	(breathe)*4
ए	e	(play)	न	na	(nut)*4
ऐ	ai	(aisle)	प	pa	(put) 5
ओ	o	(go)	फ	pha	(loophole)*5
औ	au	(loud)	ब	ba	(bin) 5
क	ka	(seek) 1	भ	bha	(abhor)*5
ख	kha	(blockhead)*1	म	ma	(much) 5
ग	ga	(get) 1	य	ya	(loyal)
घ	gha	(log hut)*1	र	ra	(red)
ङ	ṅa	(sing) 1	ल	la	(luck)
च	ca	(chunk) 2	व	va	(vase)
छ	cha	(catch him)*2	श	śa	(sure)
ज	ja	(jump) 2	ष	ṣa	(shun)
झ	jha	(hedgehog)*2	स	sa	(so)
ञ	ña	(bunch) 2	ह	ha	(hum)

•	ṁ	anusvāra	(nasalisation of preceding vowel)
:	ḥ	visarga	(aspiration of preceding vowel)
*			No exact English equivalents for these letters

1.	Guttural	–	Pronounced from throat
2.	Palatal	–	Pronounced from palate
3.	Lingual	–	Pronounced from cerebrum
4.	Dental	–	Pronounced from teeth
5.	Labial	–	Pronounced from lips

The 5ᵗʰ letter of each of the above class – called nasals – are also pronounced nasally.

A prayer is centred on a self conscious and self-judging person relating to an altar. The mode employed by the person praying is never the same, it differs from person to person. Even for a given person it differs from time to time. Prayer also can be a simple mental or oral chant or a strict elaborate Vedic ritual.

There can be three different forms of *karma*, action, in prayer: physical, *kāyika*, oral, *vācika*, and mental, *mānasa*. Performing a ritual is a physical form of prayer. Singing in praise of the Lord is an oral form of prayer while chanting a *mantra* silently is a mental form of prayer.

Prayer always has a purpose, just as any action has. You pray because you want something. Without an object of desire, there is no prayer. You may want something specific or you may want clarity of mind, *antaḥ-karaṇa-śuddhi*. You may also pray that the Lord be pleased with your prayer because you want to be in his good books; you want him to glance at you now and then. He seems to cast his blessing on others all the time, but when it comes to you, something happens, either he blinks or closes his eyes altogether.

Further, it looks as though you cannot pray for another person just as you cannot eat for another person. However, although prayer is an action, it is not like eating; it is more like bathing. Not only can you bathe, you can also bathe your child. Thus, you can pray to achieve something either for yourself or for someone else. Yet, when you pray for another person, it is still your prayer. When you see someone unhappy, who is suffering, you also suffer because you are human. You are affected by the other person's condition, and you cannot stand it. You want the other person to be happy, which really means you want to be happy. So, a prayer for others is also for the sake of your own happiness.

A prayer, therefore, is only for my sake. When I say in my prayer for my wife or child, "May my family be protected," there is an extended 'I' and that 'I' seems to be affected all the time. I am affected by everything that goes on around me, be it caused by nature or by other human beings. I need not be an American to be affected by an American being taken hostage. Every human being will be affected, once he or she knows the possible consequences of such an action. My prayer, therefore, is to help prevent or bear these experiences.

TWO RESULTS OF PRAYER

Prayer is effective, whether it is a prayer for our own sake or for another's sake. To see how such a prayer is effective and how it produces results, we have to analyse the nature of prayer itself.

One result of your prayer is immediate, *dṛṣṭa-phala*. When you pray for something, such as clarity of mind, *antaḥ-karaṇa-śuddhi*, you recognise another power higher than yourself. You are also accepting the limitation of your own power and knowledge. This is simple pragmatism. To be objective, you must know your limitations. Even when you know your limitations, often you do not want to accept them.

The fact that you can pray is wonderful because it implies an acceptance on your part, not only of your limitations, but also of the existence of a limitless source. This acceptance is a very beautiful thing; it is the immediate result of prayer. You may call it psychological if you wish, but the result is very evident. It is not easy to sit and pray, but when you do, a kind of melting happens. Otherwise, the ego will not let you sit and pray.

There is also an unseen result of prayer, *adṛṣṭa-phala*, which involves faith. The one who prays, the agent of the action of prayer, says, "This is what I want." The action and the expressed desire bring about a result, which is subtle in nature, unseen. This unseen result, which we call grace, will manifest in time. It is produced by the action of prayer and accrues to the one who prays.

KARMA IS A HUGE NETWORK OF LAWS

If you accept the law of *karma*, you can come to appreciate that most problems are brought about by the result of actions done in this life and in past lives. An acute stomach-ache or cancer, for instance, can be understood as the result of past *karma*. You could attribute the problem to heredity or genes, which is just using a different model to explain it; either way it is the same thing. If you go one step further, you would ask the reason why you were born with these particular genes. Why should you be in this situation? Why do you not have a different set of parents? If you ask these questions to a biologist, he or she will give up and say, "Go and ask a Swami. It is not my field!"

We say that there is a natural selection of parents that takes place in accordance with certain laws. If there is such a thing as the soul surviving death, there must be laws that govern the huge network of possible combinations that determine the soul's next birth. Many aspects have to be arranged such as time and place of birth, parentage, social position and culture, economic situation, and so on, all of which, in some way, affect the child who is born. Thus, each person has a particular type of *karma*.

Karma is a huge network of laws which operates purely mechanically. From the standpoint of *karma*, your stomach-ache may be a result of either past *karma* done long ago or more recently. It may be due to any number of reasons—over-eating, alcohol, or the condition of your mind—all of which can be viewed in terms of either the immediate or remote past.

If you worry about *karma*, you merely add to your misery. Therefore, worrying is useless. The past has already happened and cannot be changed. You accept it and pray. Certain damage may have been done to your stomach because of past events. If so, is there anything you can do about it now? Yes, you can pray, "Let this prayer produce results that will neutralise the past *karma*."

The law of *karma* is subtle. You do not know your past *karma*. You only know that when something occurs, it may be due to past *karma*. When extraordinary events take place and you cannot immediately account for the causes, you fall back on some past *karma* to explain them. Perhaps you win a lottery and call it good luck, or you lose something and call it bad luck; all this may be past *karma* at work. In spite of all your efforts and plans, situations that we call bad luck keep happening.

Karma unfolds every day. What you are doing right now may be due to past *karma*. It is just that you cannot see it.

Even the most die-hard atheist explains events in terms of luck. Whenever the person catches a bus, for instance, and is the last person on, before the bus starts off, he or she exclaims, "How wonderful! What luck!" Similarly, when the person misses the bus, he or she calls it bad luck.

People do miss buses in life, and there are a lot of buses. No matter how carefully we plan, at the last minute something can happen which we think of as bad luck. When such events happen, they indicate the existence of something that we are not able to lay our hands on. We do not know what it is, or how it unfolds. We only know that it keeps happening and there is some pattern to it. The law of *karma* explains that 'something'.

PRAYER NEUTRALISES ONE'S PAST
AND DAILY WRONGDOINGS

How can I neutralise the effects from the past, both immediate and remote past? There are certain options available to me, but I have to make the effort to exercise those options. Along with effort I require enthusiasm, courage, knowledge, resources, readiness and the capacity to face obstacles. However, despite all these six factors, I can miss the bus, which is why I require prayer. If these six factors are present, the Lord can help, if I pray. All six must be there for prayer to work. I cannot simply sit quietly and pray. I have to act.

There is a story about two boys who were travelling to a neighbouring village. On the way they happened to see a *Gaṇeśa* temple. One of the Hindu customs is that you should not pass a temple without offering your prayers. One boy went into the temple but the other walked on saying, "I will not go to the temple because I do not believe in all that." The boy, walking about slowly for his friend to catch him up, saw something shining on the ground. He picked it up and found it was a gold coin. Just then, he heard his friend yelling, and ran back to find out what had happened. The boy who went to the temple said, "I have been stung by a scorpion. Please help me." To which his friend replied, "This is the *prasāda*, gift, from your Lord. You went in to the temple and got a scorpion sting. Do you know what I got for not going to the temple?" He showed him the gold coin. "I got this gold coin. Why do you go to temples? It is all useless." The boy was already in pain and now his friend's words stung him to the quick. He felt that it was so unfair and was very disheartened.

As they were talking, a *sādhu* passed by. The first boy called out to him and requested his help. He told him all that had happened, the scorpion sting, and how painful it was. The *sādhu* gave him some medicine to relieve the pain. The boy then asked him, "Maharaj-ji, I went to the temple according to our custom. I have real devotion. As I was coming back, a scorpion stung me. My friend just walked past the temple and he found a gold coin on the road. What justice is this?"

The *sādhu* was an astrologer. He asked the date and time of birth of both the boys. He calculated their horoscope and told them all that had happened in their lives. He described their past events, their parents, the number of brothers and sisters and so on. Since all that he said was true, the boys had to believe him.

The *sādhu* said to the boy who had a scorpion sting, "You should have been bitten by a very poisonous cobra or met with an accident of some kind, but you got away with only a scorpion sting." To the other boy, he said, "You should have got a huge treasure, instead you had to settle for just one gold coin." The story is to illustrate the point that our efforts can affect the flow of the law of *karma*.

The purpose of prayer is to eliminate or neutralise one's daily wrongdoings. Our prayer helps to tap the grace of the limitless that is the Lord. This is one of the reasons why we are asked to pray at different times of the day, sunrise, noon, and again at sunset. Even though we may not have done anything wrong that day, there is always the past *karma* unfolding each day. Each person's *karma* is a mixture of the results of good and bad deeds, *puṇya* and *pāpa*. *Puṇya* means that which unfolds conducive or pleasant situations and *pāpa* means that which unfolds painful or unpleasant situations.

To deal with the *pāpa* that unfolds daily, minute-by-minute, we have to keep gathering *puṇya* to neutralise the *pāpa*. Prayer does this. It is not just for gaining mental clarity. By producing unseen results, it can also take care of previous wrongs.

Life is a mixture of *puṇya* and *pāpa* and brings pleasant and the unpleasant experiences. We also know that we do not dictate all terms in life and some of us may even develop our own personal philosophies to help us deal with this fact. Sometimes we may find either *puṇya* or *pāpa* coming in waves for a period of time, a few years, a few months, or a few weeks, one after the other. There may be nothing but *pāpa* for a period of time and later we may find that everything goes well, generally speaking. But within any given day, we will find there is always a combination of the two.

The morning may have been wonderful because the sun was shining, you went out to play tennis, but sprained your ankle on the court and for the next five days you could not do anything. Sometimes everything appears to be going well, but the car will not start. Alternately, the car starts, but stops in the middle of the freeway in the dead of night, six miles from a gas station; it would have been better if it had not started in the first place. Such situations may be due to omissions and commissions in the immediate past or may be due to old *pāpas*, which you want to neutralise or tone down. One unseen result can be counteracted by another unseen result. This is the purpose of prayer.

Suppose, you fall asleep with your pockets stuffed with cash and credit cards and you dream that you are starving, that you have had nothing to eat for three days, and that you have no money. Of what use is the money in your pocket? It cannot even buy you a Coke in the dream. To buy a dream Coke you need dream money. Similarly, to neutralise the unseen results gathered from previous wrong actions, you need the unseen results of prayer done in the present.

THE EFFICACY OF PRAYER

Prayer is efficacious. However, you may say that you have been praying but nothing ever happens for you.

I will counter that by saying, "If you did not pray, a lot of other things could have happened."

There was an old woman who used to tell her beads all day long. Even though she did this faithfully, she created problems for her daughter-in-law. She would stop just long enough to order the girl to do one thing or another. The poor girl, a new bride in the household, had a difficult time.

After several years of living in the same house, the daughter-in-law complained that even though her mother-in-law had done so much *japa*, there was no change in her attitude. "For the past ten years I have seen only her beads change! They have become smooth, while her mind and behaviour are as rough as they were before." I told her, "Imagine her behaviour if she had not been doing *japa*. It could have been much worse, or perhaps even impossible to live in the same house with her." The old woman's prayer, in the form of *japa*, did produce results, however small.

Prayer definitely produces result according to the law of *karma*. In any situation, an intelligent person takes into account the various factors before undertaking an action. Prayer is one such action. When we take our limitations into account and offer a prayer, the law of *karma* takes care of the results. Prayer invokes the Lord's grace.

I thought I would think aloud about what is said to be grace. Everybody uses the word. In India it is very common to say, "It is all His grace." In the Western culture also, I see the word, 'grace' being used often. The source of grace is always assumed to be the Lord, the one who is understood differently by different people. It is commonly accepted that the Lord is the source of grace, and that there is grace in one's life.

In the Indian tradition there is a lot of thinking about this grace, *anugraha, kṛpā*. We do not simply accept things without inquiry, *vicāra*. Our whole tradition is a tradition based on inquiry. Even the cultural forms are connected to religion and the religious forms are connected to the wisdom and the wisdom is born of inquiry into the source books, *śāstra-vicāra*, as a means of knowledge.

WHAT IS GRACE?

When we assume that the grace comes from Īśvara, the Lord we have to accept that He has to choose the recipient. To whom is He going to give grace today? How much? He cannot decide by a lucky dip, because the winner's name comes up due to, again, grace.

Grace is the result of *karma*. But I do not know when I did the *karma* to earn the grace. Nor do I know which *karma* is the cause for this particular grace. When I am not able to pinpoint which *karma* is responsible for this desirable thing, which is with me now, I gracefully say that it is grace. It is the result of action, *karma-phala* gracefully expressed. The result of action, *karma*, earned by me, either in this birth or in a prior birth that produces grace, is definitely not a simple *karma*, which is self-centred. It is not centred on a small self that is confined to myself the individual, or to my small family. That *karma* is not going to win grace. But when I reach out to do something to help another person, to help other living organisms in this world, which implies a self that accommodates more than the small unit called the family, then that *karma*, called *pūrta-karma*, earns grace.

In days gone by, people established things for public use like a well, a pond, even a temple of worship, a place where people can go and relax, '*vāpī-kūpa-taḍāgādi devatāyatanāni ca anna-pradānam ārāmaḥ pūrtam ityabhidhīyate.*' All these are called *pūrta-karma*. Doing any of them wins grace. Similarly, our daily prayers, rituals, and so on, also win grace. But we do not know which *karma* produces which grace.

SOURCE OF GRACE

So, grace is not something that the Lord distributes to some chosen people. We earn it as a result of our actions.

The Lord, Īśvara, of course, is very much present in it as the one who gives the result of action, *karma-phala-dātā*. The laws produce the result of action, and those laws are not separate from Īśvara. The world, *jagat* cannot be entirely different from the cause, the maker. This world has certain reality and that reality cannot come into being without some material. The maker has got to have not only some material, but also an appropriate material. The appropriateness is in terms of what is contained in the product, and also in terms of its reality. Thus, certain appropriate material is inevitable in the hands of Īśvara, the maker. And it cannot be separate from Īśvara. If the material is separate from the maker, then what separates them is space or time. However, space and time themselves are products. They are part and parcel of the *jagat*. Therefore, space does not yet exist to separate the material from Īśvara. Both the material and the maker are one and the same. The Lord is 'he' as a maker, and 'she' as the material.

The created *jagat* is more a manifestation of Īśvara than *jagat*. If he is manifest in the form of the *jagat*, which includes your body-mind-sense complex, then there is no question of the material being separate from Īśvara. It is a very important fact to know.

The maker and the material being identical, and the world being non-separate from the Lord, the laws that are also the Lord produce the results of action. While some of these laws are partially known to me, there are many laws that are totally unknown to me. But I do know that the laws being what they are do not err. They do not transgress themselves. Therefore, I can relax in the awareness that the laws cannot cheat me. In keeping with the laws, for all those special actions that I have done, I have earned something favourable called *puṇya*. But I cannot pinpoint the *karma* that brought this to me. In life if I have to be at the right place at the right time, I cannot say what accounts for that happening.

I do not know whether it is true, but definitely most of you think that being in America, you are at the right place. Some of the newcomers, however, think they are not here at the right time, unless they are engaged in an Internet start-up company and can sell it for a windfall. Others always think that they have come a little late. They are at the right place, but at the wrong time. To be at the right place at the right time is not in our hands. It is very funny how we have a lot of plans. If you want to make God laugh all you have to do is tell him your plans for the future!

One does not call all the shots. One's whole life is a percentage game, like baseball. When this kind of human predicament is there, the self-conscious human being recognizes his or her helplessness. When one recognizes one's helplessness and then one finds oneself in favourable situations, the pragmatic, objective human being cannot but recognise and acknowledge something unknown which shaped this situation in his or her favour.

RECOGNISING GRACE

People who acknowledge grace are objective people. They are pragmatic. Grace is a graceful acceptance of a situation. It is also grace that keeps you going. You see the green light and drive on, assuming that the other person saw the red light. This assumption is purely rooted in grace because you have no basis to make such an assumption. It is pure trust. The other person may be seeing many lights, because he had one too many Lights, Bud Light.[1] How do you know that even after having seen the red light he will not drive through it? When you breathe out, definitely there is the hope that you will breath in, and the air that you breathed out will come back. If you have a doubt you will try not to breathe out.

---

[1] Name of a beer in the United States.

When you breathe out, hoping the breath will come back, there is the possibility that it may not come back at all!

Look at this pumping heart. It is the greatest blessing. Even though it is a simple pump, it is a sturdy pump. It started even before you were born, before you had seen the light of day. And it has been pumping all the time without any rest. If I ask you to clench your fist and open it again for fifteen minutes, after ten minutes you want to have a tea break. But this heart has got to work all the time. It has no respite at all. Even if you go into a coma it goes on. It is an amazing organ. It is just tissues, but definitely between the lub and dub I see certain grace. It is grace because, after lub there need not be a dub at all. It can be lublub. It is lub grace dub, grace lub grace dub.

When this possibility of death is kept away to keep our life going, we can say there is grace. It is not something that visits us occasionally. It is there very much with us between the lub and the dub.

That we are alive is a miracle. That we are still sane is another miracle. That we remain married and each one admires the other is the miracle of miracles. It is called *āścarya*, a wonder. That we are blessed with children is another miracle. Every time we go out and come back in one piece, it is a miracle. Almost everyday we hear of accidents, earthquakes and volcanic eruptions. That we are able to retain our sanity in spite of a disturbing front-page in the morning tabloid is grace. The grace seems to work overtime. It is such a beautiful thing to recognise the miracle of living. Every moment is a reality that unfolds something precious to us and if we are with the moment, we recognise the meaning and profundity of living.

EARNING GRACE BY EXERCISING THE WILL

Actions of prayer and actions that reach out earn us grace. Most of us are busy day after day with our time consumed by our reactions, and our reactions to reactions. First we react in anger and say things which are inappropriate. Then, we regret what we said. That can trigger a series of reactions. It is through actions alone that we can express ourselves.

What really makes you different from any other living being on this planet is your capacity to choose. That capacity to choose and do is what is called free will. If a cow is a vegetarian it is not by choice, but if you are one, it is by choice. That is will. You choose.

The freedom that your will seems to have is often inhibited by external and internal pressures. You are in a situation where you are called upon to do something appropriate which you may not like to do. You have to do it because it is duty. The concept of duty imposes a pressure on you unless you love to do what needs to be done. If you have to do it, whether you like it, then it is better to learn to like it.

Free will becomes a hostage in the hands of your own likes and dislikes, *rāga-dveṣa*. Even an act of giving does not come from your heart. It is because you are pressurised. The giving is more to get rid of your wretchedness than to help the person. This is not giving. You have to give with all your heart; only then is there grace. There is no other way of earning grace. It has to come out of you. You are as much as you think you are. You can have millions of dollars and still feel small because you cannot open up. A rich person is one who can willingly give what he or she has. Here is a person begging for his living. He has his lunch–left with one rupee. When another beggar comes to him and says, "I am hungry," he gives away that one rupee. He is the rich man, not the millionaire who cannot part with a penny.

Only when you reach out and do something, do you win grace. Prayer also is like that. It is not that easy to pray and it is very difficult to pray heartily. The ego will not let that happen. Even though you know that you are helpless, still, there is something that makes you incapable of praying. Why? It is often found to be an authority problem.

Grace is something you have to tap. It is not distributed by God. It is like underground water in that you have to tap it, and the tapping is done by action alone. Grace is always there. It is a possibility like any other possibility.

There are many things that are manifest, surfaced, in this universe. There are also many possibilities lying there for you to tap. Every piece of new software was a possibility. Every piece of hardware was a possibility. Grace is another possibility. People think that when one is in trouble one will pray. No, when you are in trouble you hit your head on the wall. You phone somebody and cry. Or you go on a buying spree but you do not pray because of pressure.

Prayer is a deliberate action where the free will is totally free; an uninhibited free will. It is that kind of action that wins grace. This is why you say, "I perform this *karma* to win the grace of Parameśvara, *śri parameśvara-prītyartham aham idaṁ kariṣye*. It is not to please Īśvara.

Besides the grace of Īśvara, *īśvara-kṛpā*, there is *guru-kṛpā*. There is also *śāstra-kṛpā*. The *guru* may be there, but when you pick up the book you go to sleep. The *śāstra* has to reveal itself. That is also Īśvara's grace, but in terms of *śāstra*.

Finally, there is *ātma-kṛpā*—you should be deserving of grace. You need to use your free will and earn it. When it is there, recognise it.

In the eyes of your child you can see the grace. When you say a good word there is grace flowing. When you are aware of grace, your whole life is one of grace. That is *ātma-kṛpā*.

Human life can become very complex if one does not keep it simple. There are enough reasons to make your life complex, but there are enough reasons, also, for you to be more humble, to be simple. If you look at yourself as one who is in charge of everything, then you will have to face yourself and the situations with regret, with a sense of guilt, for you do not control all the situations. You try. You try hard to control situations. You cannot. You cannot even control your weight, what to talk of situations. I am not talking about grey hair if there is hair. There, you have no control whatsoever. If in aging you have no control what control can you have in changing people? It is impossible.

Each one has some agenda for everybody else. You do not really pause and think that: "If I have an agenda for everybody in my life, will they not have an agenda for me?" They are bound to have. If you analyse others' agenda, then you will have new problems to deal with. You will feel that nobody understands you. That is exactly what others also think; that you do not understand them. So, problems become more and more complex when you do not understand that you cannot change people and you do not call all the shots.

Life is a percentage game. To make any headway you have to be at the right place at the right time, and that is not possible, for it is not under your control. Therefore, you just remain humble. This does not mean subservience, but an enlightened humbleness, that comes out of your appreciation of your own capacities, skills, virtues, and, at the same time, your limitations.

The limitations you have are greater than the skills that you are endowed with. So, what you cannot do is much greater than what you can. Naturally, therefore, what you can do is also given. It is not something that you have created after coming into the world. The very body is given to you. Your mind and the senses are given to you. The capacity to know is given to you. An infrastructure in which you can create things is given to you. The laws that you can explore and use to invent are also given to you. Everything, in fact, is given to you. What you cannot do is a given fact with which you have to live with, and, of course, you have to face it. It is not an easy thing. People always have reasons to complain. When you have nothing else to complain about, you can always say, "I have no wings." It is the same thing with reference to others also.

You do not look for what others have. You always look for what they do not have, what you think they should have, or should not have. It is amazing how we look at people and relate to them. We invite problems. This is what I call a 'proof-reader's psychology,' looking for the mistakes, the omissions, as well as the commissions of others. It is a particular psychology. It makes your life complex, and more and more complex as days pass by, and years pass by. When you celebrate a New Year, you should also know that one year has gone. That means you are aging.

Time is such a severe force. It ages you. It does not make any exceptions, even the mountains. It is severe and ubiquitous, and is not going to leave anybody, anywhere, out of its handiwork. Every wrinkle you have is the handiwork of time. Therefore, age you will. It is certain. But you can celebrate a New Year if you have grown up by one year. Everybody ages, but if, in one year, you have grown up, if you have one more year of inner growth, you can celebrate. This growth can only take place by your own initiative.

I look upon growth not in terms of skills and so on, even though they also characterise one's growth, one's accomplishments, but the real growth is in how simple one has made one's life. From being complex one has to make it simple. When I say 'simple' I do not mean that you have to live in a hut. Even in a hut you can lead a complex life. I know a person who moved from a mansion to a cottage. He took all the people there to show how simple he lived, and threw parties there. I am not proposing that you should cut anything down; you just have to be simple. While being simple and avoiding complexity you need to be very alert. Just with time, life becomes very complex with every passing year. However, emotionally you can be simple and more cheerful. Physically you will be aging, but when you are growing emotionally in the reverse proportion, then you can celebrate. You can keep your life simple because it is simple. It is very simple.

I see a world and it is full of possibilities. It has many probabilities, not just possibilities, and they are all open for me. I am self-conscious, and because of that I can make it complex. I make it complex because all the conditions are there for me to have complexes. To keep it simple I need to be alert, appreciate my own limitations and my virtues. Some people appreciate their limitations and their virtues. Some others appreciate only their limitations and not their virtues. There are others who do not want to acknowledge their limitations because they cannot handle that. Since, I am conscious of myself with the innate intelligence, I need to be aware of the limitations and the endowments given to me. I can then be humble. This enlightened humbleness makes me very prayerful.

Ambitions are beautiful and they are given to you. Only a human being can have such ambitions. An ambition being what it is, you can fulfil them, or you need not fulfil them. On New Year's day, you may have certain goals that need to be accomplished. May be this is a good time to think about that. It is good to know all the things you want, and to think about what you want ultimately.

What are the things you want to accomplish in the near future? You need to have some clarity. But remember one thing. These are things that you want, these are the ambitions that you have; you may fulfil them, you may not be able to fulfil them. If you do not fulfil them, that does not make you a failure. It only confirms the fact that it is not possible to fulfil all wants. That is a fact because you are limited.

Having done all the homework, there are hidden variables. There is nothing you can do about them. But if you do not do anything about them, there may be any number of obstacles that can come in the way of your accomplishing your goals. If you do not do anything about them, because you think you cannot, that really makes you helpless. That will definitely stagnate your efforts, because it will inhibit your thinking, and also your clarity. Therefore, you have to acknowledge and address the hidden variables as well. How to address them? Since you do not know what the hidden variables are, you can offer a prayer for the success of your pursuit without impediment. Prayer is a deliberate *karma* you undertake to address the hidden variables.

You pray and you are prayerful. To pray is easy. In a given time and place you pray. But to be prayerful you have to change. There can be a lot of difference between a person who is prayerful and a person who prays at a given time. You may pray at a given time, and the rest of the time prey on others. That is an entirely different thing altogether. To pray at a given time is also important, but, then, you should be prayerful until you sit for prayer again. The day is spent prayerfully.

Life has to be prayerful. Being prayerful means having an awareness of everything that is given, and the awareness of a Giver. More the awareness you have of the presence of Īśvara as the giver and the given, the more prayerful you are.

If you analyse it, nobody can say that he or she is lonely, and yet everybody feels lonely. It is because you feel that you are not understood. "Nobody wants me, nobody likes me, and I want people to understand me, to claim me." It is very childish. If a child says this, it is valid. If an adult says it, we consider it childish.

In this vast world, how can you feel lonely? But you do feel lonely because, as a child, perhaps, you felt that you were not understood, not included. That is the problem. But then, you may find that one person, a therapist, perhaps, understands you. It is possible, but that person also needs to be understood by others. And he or she also needs to understand himself or herself a lot. You cannot pretend to be God, and also say, now and then, "I am sorry. I did not mean that at all." When the therapist says sorry, naturally, your trust in him or her becomes very limited, and the validation from the therapist is not going to be as complete for you. Even then, the therapist will validate you because the person is paid for that. The therapist is a specialist and knows exactly what he or she has to do as a therapist. The therapist will validate you; there is no question about that. But the problem is, you have an eroded trust. You have pain inside. The people whom you thought were infallible proved to be fallible. The therapist also is fallible. Therefore, you cannot even say, "My therapist totally understands me, validates me."

So, I have to appoint a therapist for myself in whose eyes I will be totally, absolutely validated. That person is not going to come by. That conscious being is what we call the Giver, the Lord, and the one who is all-knowledge. In his eyes, therefore, I am always validated because he is all-knowledge. I am not going to spring any surprise on him. If you cannot surprise the Lord, then it means he is all-knowledge. If you are going to surprise somebody, then he or she is small knowing. If I am not a surprise to anyone, then I am exactly what I could be. In no other way could I be. That is the rigor of the law or order.

You are exactly as you should be at this time and place. In your life, this is exactly what you are expected to be at this time and place. The Lord is the only one who knows it. And in order to say this, you have to know the Lord to be so. You are appreciating an omniscient being in whose knowledge you are totally accepted. You do not need anybody else to approve of you, to accept you.

You need not ask the Lord, " O Lord please accept me. I may have many omissions and commissions, but please accept me." The Lord is not a limited individual, like an uncle. In your vision of Īśvara, you are totally acceptable. It is not enough to say that in the vision of Īśvara you are acceptable. That is all 'iffy' because it depends on how much you understand Īśvara. It is not enough to say that God is infallible. You have to discover the infallible is God. In his vision you are totally acceptable. There you can relax.

The one who counts is only the Lord. When I say that everything is non-separate from the Lord, then all that counts is one. In his presence I am totally acceptable. That I am acceptable in his vision is my understanding, and that understanding is a must. I have to see that I am an individual given this body-mind-sense complex, and as an individual I have limitations, I have virtues. Both I acknowledge, and I am prayerful. I pray for the things I want, and one of the things I pray for is to be prayerful.

Thus, the whole life is one of prayerfulness. I can look back and say that time, of course, rung out, but it brought in a lot for me. So, I can say it was a very good year, and I look forward to the next year, because in growth there is a joy. In simplicity there is joy.

The simpler you are, more the people will love you because people are complex. Everybody has lots of problems. Therefore, they look for a simple person. People want to relate to a simple person, not a simpleton, but a simple person who is a wise person. If a wise person is not simple then he is not wise, he is 'otherwise'. The simpler you are, more profound are the things that you come to discover when you pray, "Let my life be prayerful."

Oṁ tat sat

Books by Swami Dayananda Saraswati

Public Talk Series :

1. Living Intelligently
2. Successful Living
3. Need for Cognitive Change
4. Discovering Love
5. The Value of Values
6. Vedic View and Way of Life

Upaniṣad Series :

7. Muṇḍakopaniṣad
8. Kenopaniṣad

Text Translation Series :

9. Śrīmad Bhagavad Gītā
   (Text with roman transliteration and English translation)
10. Śrī Rudram
    (Text in Sanskrit with transliteration, word-to-word and verse meaning along with an elaborate commentary in English)

Stotra Series :

11. Dīpārādhanā
12. Prayer Guide
    (With explanations of several Mantras, Stotras, Kirtans and Religious Festivals)

Essays :

Exploring Vedanta Series : (vākyavicāra)

Books translated in other languages and in English based on Swami Dayananda Saraswati's Original Exposition

Kannada

Hindi

DISTRIBUTED BY MOTILAL BANARSIDASS WORLDWIDE

Also available at :

ARSHA VIDYA RESEARCH
AND PUBLICATION TRUST
32/4 Sir Desika Road
Mylapore Chennai 600 004
Telefax   : 044 - 2499 7131
Email   : avrandpc@gmail.com

ARSHA VIDYA GURUKULAM
Anaikatti P.O.
Coimbatore 641 108
Ph   : 0422 - 2657001
Fax   : 0422 - 2657002
Email   : office@arshavidya.in

ARSHA VIDYA GURUKULAM
P.O.Box 1059. Pennsylvania
PA 18353, USA.
Ph   : 001-570-992-2339
Email   : avp@epix.net

SWAMI DAYANANDA ASHRAM
Purani Jhadi, P.B. No. 30
Rishikesh, Uttaranchal 249 201
Telefax : 0135-2430769
Email   : ashrambookstore@yahoo.com

AND IN ALL THE LEADING BOOK STORES, INDIA